3 1994 01329 7764

SANTA ANA PUBLIC LIBRARY
NEWHOPE BRANCH

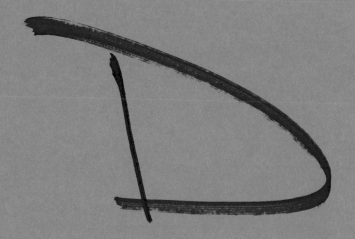

BIOGRAPHIES

ABRAHAM LINCOLN
LAWYER, PRESIDENT, EMANCIPATOR

Written by Pamela Hill Nettleton
Illustrated by Becky Shipe

Special thanks to our advisers for their expertise:

Gregory L. Kaster, Ph.D., Chair, Department of History
Gustavus Adolphus College, St. Peter, Minnesota

Susan Kesselring, M.A., Literacy Educator
Rosemount–Apple Valley–Eagan (Minnesota) School District

PICTURE WINDOW BOOKS
MINNEAPOLIS, MINNESOTA

J B LINCOLN, A. NET
Nettleton, Pamela Hill.
Abraham Lincoln
31994013297764

Managing Editor: Bob Temple
Creative Director: Terri Foley
Editor: Peggy Henrikson
Editorial Adviser: Andrea Cascardi
Copy Editor: Laurie Kahn
Page production: The Design Lab
The illustrations in this book were rendered digitally.

PICTURE WINDOW BOOKS
5115 Excelsior Boulevard
Suite 232
Minneapolis, MN 55416
1-877-845-8392
www.picturewindowbooks.com

Copyright © 2004 by Picture Window Books
All rights reserved. No part of this book may be reproduced
without written permission from the publisher. The publisher
takes no responsibility for the use of any of the materials or
methods described in this book, nor for the products thereof.

Printed in the United States of America.

Library of Congress Cataloging-in-Publication Data
Nettleton, Pamela Hill.
Abraham Lincoln : lawyer, president, emancipator / written by Pamela Hill Nettleton ;
illustrated by Becky Shipe.
p. cm. — (Biographies)
Summary: A brief biography that highlights some important events in the life of the man
who was President during the Civil War.
Includes bibliographical references (p.) and index.
ISBN 1-4048-0185-5
1. Lincoln, Abraham, 1809–1865–Juvenile literature. 2. Presidents–United States–
Biography–Juvenile literature. [1. Lincoln, Abraham, 1809–1865. 2. Presidents.]
I. Shipe, Becky, 1977– ill. II. Title.
E457.905 .N48 2003
973.7'092–dc21   2003004135

Abraham Lincoln faced many great challenges in his life. No matter how difficult they were, he never gave up. He cared about people, and he was a great leader. As the 16th president of the United States, Abe helped change history with his caring ways and his powerful words and actions.

This is the story of Abraham Lincoln.

Abraham Lincoln was born on a farm in Kentucky in 1809. When Abe was seven, the family moved west to Indiana. The Lincolns were poor, but they worked hard. When Abe was only eight, he could swing an ax.

He helped his father cut down trees to clear fields for farming. They built a new log cabin and put up fences.

Abe could not go to school very often. In fact, if you added up all the days he went to school, it would total less than one year. His family needed him to chop wood and do chores. But Abe really wanted to learn. He spent a lot of his free time reading.

Books and paper were hard to find.
Sometimes Abe wrote on wood with a knife.

Abe's mother, Nancy Hanks Lincoln, died when Abe was nine. A year later, his father married Sarah Bush Johnston. She became Abe's stepmother. Abe was sad that his mother had died, but he liked his stepmother.

Abe's mother died from drinking bad milk. The milk came from a cow that had eaten poisonous plants.

When Abe was 21 years old,
the family moved again to find a better life
in Illinois. They had to start over,
clearing land and building a cabin.

Abe tried many jobs. He worked on riverboats.
He worked in a store. He split wood to make fence rails.
He was very tall and thin, but he was strong.

People liked Abe. He told stories that made them laugh. He was friendly and kind, and he told the truth.

Abe's nickname was Honest Abe.

When Abe was 22, his family moved again, but he didn't go. He went to New Orleans, Louisiana, on one of his riverboat trips. There he saw a slave market for the first time, and he didn't like it. People were buying black slaves. The slaves had chains on their hands and feet.

During the early years of America, many black people were sold as slaves. Slave owners made their slaves work hard. Slaves got food, clothing, and housing, but no pay. They had to follow their owners' wishes.

Abe returned to Illinois and settled in New Salem. He ran for the state legislature but lost. Again he tried many jobs, such as owning a store, mapping land, and being postmaster. But he liked politics and finally was elected to the Illinois House of Representatives in 1834. He also studied to become a lawyer. The frontier had no law schools, so Abe made up homework for himself. He studied hard and became a lawyer in 1836.

Abe sometimes walked 20 miles from his home in New Salem to Springfield to borrow books.

Abe was elected to the Illinois legislature three more times. Then, in 1846, he was elected to represent Illinois in Congress in Washington, D.C. Later, Abe returned to Illinois and became one of the state's best lawyers.

Abe married a lively woman named Mary Todd in 1842. They had four sons, but three of them died young. This made Abe and his wife very sad for many years.

Abe became interested in politics again because of slavery. Some states in the South allowed it. States in the North did not. Abe and Senator Stephen Douglas from Illinois argued about this. Was it right to own slaves? Lincoln said no. Douglas said each state should decide.

Many people heard about the debates between Lincoln and Douglas. Some thought Abe would make a good president. But people in the South did not like his ideas about slavery.

Abe decided to run for president, and he was elected in 1860. By the time he started the job, seven Southern states had joined together and formed their own government. Four others followed. A few months later, the North and South were fighting what came to be called the Civil War.

The Southern states called themselves the Confederate States of America.

Abe wanted the country to stop fighting. He also wanted to stop the spread of slavery. He wrote and spoke boldly for peace and for unity in the country.

If the South had won the Civil War, the United States might be two countries today.

As president, Abe made a ruling in 1863 called the
Emancipation Proclamation. This ruling changed
the Civil War. At first, the purpose of the war was
to keep the North and South together. Abe's ruling made
it a war to free the slaves as well. Slaves in the South were
allowed to join the army or navy in the North and be free.
Many did, and it greatly helped the North.

After the big Civil War battle at Gettysburg, Pennsylvania, Abe made a famous speech called the Gettysburg Address. He spoke for only two minutes, but his wise words are still remembered. He said the nation should stand for freedom and equality.

Executive Mansion
Washington

Four score and seven years ago our fathers brought forth, upon this continent, a new nation, conceived in liberty, and dedicated to the proposition that "all men are created equal."

The Lincoln Memorial was built
in Washington, D.C.,
to honor Abraham Lincoln.

Thousands of people died in the Civil War. Finally, the North won a major battle on April 9, 1865. Abe hoped the war would soon be over. He wanted the country to heal and become a strong nation.

Five days later, Abe was watching a play at Ford's Theatre. A man named John Wilkes Booth shot Abe in the back of the head. John was angry that the South was losing the war, and he blamed Abe. Abe died on April 15, 1865. Many people throughout the country mourned his death. In May, the war ended with a victory for the North. This meant that Abe's wish for a united country came true.

Today, many people think of Abraham Lincoln as one of the greatest Americans.

THE LIFE OF ABRAHAM LINCOLN

1809   Born on February 12 in Hardin County, Kentucky

1834   Elected to the Illinois government (House of Representatives)

1836   Became a lawyer

1842   Married Mary Todd

1846   Was elected to represent Illinois in Congress in Washington, D.C.

1858   Debated against Stephen Douglas and got lots of attention

1860   Was elected the 16th president of the United States and took up
his duties in February of 1861

1861   The Civil War began in April.

1863   Wrote the Emancipation Proclamation and gave the Gettysburg Address

1865   Was shot and died the next day, April 15

DID YOU KNOW?

- Abraham Lincoln did not have a middle name.

- Abe was 6 feet 4 inches (2 meters) tall—the tallest U.S. president so far.

- Abe earned $25,000 a year as president. In 2001, the president's salary was set at $400,000.

- Abe's Emancipation Proclamation led Congress to pass the 13th Amendment to the Constitution. This amendment ended slavery in the United States for good. It was passed in 1865, about eight months after Abe was killed.

- After John Wilkes Booth shot Abe, he jumped down to the stage and broke his leg. He still got away, but he was caught and killed 12 days later.

- Abe liked to tell stories and jokes. He loved to ask his sons, "How many legs would a dog have if you called its tail a leg?" His sons would answer, "Five!" Then Abe would say, "No, it would have only four. Calling a tail a leg does not make it a leg."

GLOSSARY

amendment (uh-MEND-muhnt)—a change or addition to a law or group of laws

Congress (KONG-griss)—the group in the United States government that makes laws

constitution (kon-stuh-TOO-shuhn)—the written ideas and laws upon which a government is based

debate (di-BATE)—a discussion between two sides with different ways of thinking on a subject. Each side tries to convince people that it is right.

elect (i-LEKT)—to choose by voting

emancipation (i-man-si-PAY-shuhn)—freedom from slavery or control

emancipator (i-MAN-si-pay-tur)—someone who frees others from slavery or control

proclamation (prah-cluh-MAY-shuhn)—a public announcement or statement

representative (rep-ri-ZEN-tuh-tiv)—someone who is chosen to act or speak for others

slavery (SLAY-vur-ee)—the practice of owning other people called slaves. Slaves had to do what their owners told them to do. They were not free.

TO LEARN MORE

At the Library

Blashfield, Jean F. *Abraham Lincoln.* Minneapolis: Compass Point Books, 2002.

Freedman, Russell. *Lincoln: A Photobiography.* New York: Clarion Books, 1987.

Heinrichs, Ann. *The Emancipation Proclamation.* Minneapolis: Compass Point Books, 2002.

Marrin, Albert. *Commander in Chief Abraham Lincoln and the Civil War.* New York: Dutton Children's Books, 1997.

Schaefer, Lola M. *Abraham Lincoln.* Mankato, Minn.: Pebble Books/Capstone Press, 1999.

On the Web

ABRAHAM LINCOLN PRESIDENTIAL LIBRARY & MUSEUM: KIDS PAGE

Tells about Lincoln's life and his family. Includes historical sites and links to more information
http://www.alincoln-library.com/Apps/kids/default.asp

LINCOLN/NET

For facts about the life and times of Abraham Lincoln and links to his writings
http://lincoln.lib.niu.edu/aboutinfo.html

FACT HOUND

Fact Hound offers a safe, fun way to find Web sites related to this book. All of the sites on Fact Hound have been researched by our staff.
http://www.facthound.com

1. Visit the Fact Hound home page.
2. Enter a search word related to this book, or type in this special code: 1404801855.
3. Click on the FETCH IT button.

Your trusty Fact Hound will fetch the best sites for you!

On a Trip

NATIONAL PARK SERVICE:
LINCOLN HOME NATIONAL HISTORIC SITE
426 South Seventh Street (Visitor Center)
Springfield, IL 62701-1905
(217) 492-4241, Ext. 221
http://www.nps.gov/liho

INDEX